D1713140

Zebra

Poems by

Nadine S. St. Louis

Marsh River Editions

First Edition

"Pretending to Be Sinéad O'Connor" appeared in
Kalliope: A Journal of Women's Literature and Art.

"Epiphany" appeared in *Poetica Grandmatica.*

Cover photograph by
Sharp Photo & Portrait
3306 Mall Drive
Eau Claire, WI 54701

ISBN 978-0-9772768-5-1
Publisher/Editor Linda Aschbrenner
Printed by Heinzen Printing Inc., Marshfield, Wisconsin

Marsh River Editions
M233 Marsh Road
Marshfield, WI 54449
marshrivereditions.com

Dedication

To Bob

To Leigh and Jason

To Faith, Shannon, and Zoë

and to all those other family, friends,
and physicians who have so devotedly woven
the lifeline that has kept me afloat in heavy seas

Contents

Zebra

*Physicians have been taught to expect
the ordinary, not the rare, condition—
to look for horses, not zebras. Sometimes,
however, a zebra does appear.*

— NSS

Breakaway

She was brought up to think
inside the box, to color inside
the lines: *best of all possible worlds;*
if it ain't broke, don't fix it;
ours not to reason why. . . .
Now you ask her to predict
where the world is going
in a hundred years: "'Way
away from me, but maybe
I still have some time," she says,
even as she kicks the first slat
off the side of the box
and starts scribbling on the walls.

Diagnostic

with thanks to Naomi Shihab Nye

You'll spend a long time waiting,
they said, *so bring a book.* I brought
poetry, pensive words of a gentle warrior.

In the beginning was the word.

Nine days of corridors and chairs,
hard-edged beige rooms with metal
tables, ponderous machines, stethoscopes,
isotopes, exotic liquids, dry air. Waiting

and reading I keep coming back
to two poems. In one the poet honors
a grandmother I wish I'd known,
patient desert dweller whose language
I do not speak, whose spirit
is healing water.

In the other she thanks another poet—
I guess at the name—whose words buoy her
"like a raft," and I know the feeling
because her words are bearing me up,
and I look up and say again *Yes.*

In yet another enameled room,
baring a too-familiar vein, I receive
into my hand a soft gauze cylinder
and dutifully clench it into my fist.

Magnetic Resonance

Just let yourself lean back.
Slip into place. We'll read
your body like a credit card.

But what about the sound?
It's a classical robot jam—dig it!

Ball-peen hammer section opens,
andante, tapping out mellow
introduction, long rests.
Enter two baritone electric drills
antiphonal, statement
and response. Longer rest.

Repeat. Repeat.

Next breath, after a cool drill riff,
crescendo, oscillators take over
con brio, telling a joke, Spike
Joneses of machine music,
alto and bass, with percussion
by runaway metronome, *giocoso.*
Bass and then again alto
buzzers finish the set, *fortissimo;*
The metronome fades as bamboo
water pipes pick up the beat, *mezzo-
staccato,* drop by drop, those folk
tale tellers of the robot world,
theirs an old theme. Stay
quiet now; relax into the silence.
The band'll be right back.

CAT Scan

Sort of an evangelical experience,
arms up in the air—hallelujah!—
face to heaven, or at least the ceiling glows.
One little needle slide and a voice, male,
telling you *Hold your breath* (tempting to
count/two/three)—*breathe*—as you glide
feet first through the magic ring, glide
back out: this was only a test.

Now they get serious. Mystic liquid
(*You'll feel hot, get some nether urgency.*
Yes, but not the kind they mean. This
is one sexy rush for just an instant, quite
UN-evangelical)—hallelujah

time again. Pierce the ring; *hold*
your breath he says again (two/three).
Breathe. Stiff-held body in and out, in
and out of the ring. The breathing. The rush.

Not bad, machine, not too bad,
if only 35 seconds. And not once
did anybody even mention the cat.

Medical Imaging

You learn to walk the corridors
like a tightrope, eyes fixed
on some lithe figure in kaleidoscope scrubs
waiting with pen and clipboard
or needle or liter measure of substance
artificial or naturally occurring.

The rooms are always dim
geometries of heavy equipment,
bombsights in myriad configurations,
magic circles and squares of clockwork.

Yet in this room, Brunhilde's
voluptuous apron—a domestic touch—
hangs leaden on the wall,
aubergine piped in black,
distracting for just a moment until
you remember her ring of fire,
the way she rode singing back
to the immortals. You wonder
who would notice if you tried your voice.

Confusion to the Enemy

"So rare," the white coats agree, though
you'd consider the trait more satisfying
in love and song than physiology.
But when you find yourself turning
into a conference paper, what's left
but to honor the distinction, take up
your own cause: stand tough, think tall,
look straight into the eye of the beast.

Beast, what a big, red eye you have.
The better to make you burn, my dear.

Smug, that's what it is, too used
to driving its prey to the wall
with a glare from that scorching eye.

You know you can't allow such easy victory,
must turn back the monster on itself,
so you raise your defiant glass to damp the fire—
My turn to name the poison, Beast.
You speak the unspeakable, take rarity
as a virtue. You drink deep.

Sic Transit

Just inside the big revolving doors
half a hundred wheelchairs wait, or more,
just say the word. Have a seat.
They'll summon a cheery helper to push,
or your friend there can do the job.
All along the broad corridors, building
to building, you'll see cautious husbands,
wives, blue-jacketed volunteers
propelling their charges with almost
sacerdotal care, gentle, deliberate.

Not my daughter.

       Now there's a woman
who knows how to motivate
a pair of wheels. If I have to go
by chair, she's the one
I want at my back, whisking
through doorways, trotting down ramps,
negotiating the corridors at a speed
that makes my hair blow.
Passersby stare and catch their breath,
but she and I laugh. That's the fuel
that makes us both run smoothly
even on the rockiest days.

Heavy Metal and
the Reciprocal Universe

Platinum and its analogues slip silent
precious poison through your veins,
and the taste of sour metal blooms.

Who can resist asking what gift
calls up this bane, resist thinking
the smiles of one god

will raise the wrath of another?
Take lone, emaciated Phineas:
Apollo endowed him with prophecy,

made him observer of worlds,
model builder, truth teller
who learned to hold life

at a new angle, disclose its secret
lights and shadows.

        But Zeus, ever lord
of secrets, demanded tighter security,

sent harpies to foul the very bread
in the old man's hands, stinking polluters
to remind him of a god's might.

Is theirs the same vile breath swirling

at the back of your throat, cold echo
of the body's rage smoldering deeper down?

It took the sons of Boreas, North Wind,
to drive away the harpies.
Phineas kept his voice. His rescue

bodes well; his endurance heartens.
Still, you can't help wondering how long
it takes the wind to turn.

On Being Given a Book
of Poetry Mourning
All Those Who Have Not
Survived Cancer

I honor them, of course; we all do.
We all have known so many. Every day
we hesitate through the gaps
where they stood.

But this book belongs
to the uninvaded, those
with the luxury of contemplating
death on a theoretical level, tidily
balanced against, say, beauty,
fame, or honor. It is not for the ones
who wake in deep night swearing
they see a deeper shadow biding.

Think of it as an exercise
in tightwire walking.
Be an observer: study the physics,
catalog the heights, the tensions,
the breath-clutching thrills, the accidents
with and without a net, all neat,
uncomplicated, both feet on the ground.

But practice the art and you set your feet
onto support so slender it could cut.
The world beneath turns void and falls away.

Objective reality is—has to be—
that one slim wire that extends no room
for doubt. Concentration is everything.

So thank you, my friend, for the thought;
forgive me if I decline your gift.
My nights are too shaded just now,
my wire too thin.

Pretending to Be Sinéad O'Connor

Helping me take back control, Faith
shaved my head. The hair
had only begun to fall, but we filled
the house with a power of women, raised
toasts in champagne, and dropped
tress upon tress into a handmade bowl
marked with the Chinese character
for *voluptuous*. In a magic circle
we sang songs, read poems, told
our stories in the old way.
We tried on wigs and scarves,
cried a little, and laughed,
then scattered to our separate lives.

The heavy metal that did in my hair
still sings off key through my veins
but now I'm discovering the freedom
of transformation: for formal occasions
I wear the Rosie Clooney wig, ash blonde
with just a hint of frost; for casual
I have the scarves, gypsy knotted,
turban wrapped. When I feel
like insurrection, though,
I bypass all those and show the world
bare reality; I dare
to startle, shock, unnerve.
I do not hide the naked truth.

Harmonics

today at last
I understood
that wheelbarrow
(red) and
those chickens

seeing our white car
beneath bright crimson
October oak

how colors sing

On Cutting Ladies in Two

for the magician and his assistants

Having stepped into the light with the magician,
having been cut in half with glittering
domestic steel, having slipped deep
into the shadow and emerged
rejoined with a wave of the gloved hand

(Henry VIII, they say, imported the finest
French blade, a technical marvel of the time,
to do the honors for Anne Boleyn,
but no matter that she hoped for a miracle,
she remained woman apart)

you return, besieged liver freed
of its invader, liberated, though
you cannot speak for your emotions.

(The liver in Anne's time was believed
seat of the emotions, shaper of will,
smothering reason with its fume,
burning, burning.)

For now you live on a dusty edge
through long, sleepless nights
though these too you know shall pass.

(You do not bear the weight

*of a country's fate
or a king's pleasure.)*

Eyes tight against the dark
you ponder briefly your own
moment in history. Soon enough
you will stand and reflect
in the sun rising how fine the line
between science and magic,
how much a matter of timing.

Being Alice

Some days you can happily
wander the town, sit chatting
at civilized tea tables, take the air.
Others, you seem to fall
straight down the rabbit hole,
never quite hitting bottom, just
slamming into the sides now and then.

Bad Hair Days

When I was six and had scarlet fever
or it might have been polio, gone from child
to furnace in a day, my hair
started to fall out from the heat,
so Mother cut it. No more
waist-length braids and curls. She cried.
I cried. We consoled ourselves saying,
"It'll grow," the way we did
later when a haircut went wrong—
and it did, but never again long enough
to sit on. From Rapunzel to Lauren Bacall.

Six decades after, I watched history
repeat like an absent-minded angel,
heavy metal doing the damage.
This time when the hair started to fall,
we, the women, held a Ritual Head Shaving,
assuring ourselves it would grow back.
"Yes, but I'll bet it'll come back white,"
I said, not having seen the real thing
in twenty years. "And curly," thus
a prophetic friend who'd been there.
"Once it gets long enough," I promised
to the grandchildren's delight,
"I'll spike it"—and I would too,
except for the curls. Every morning
I start out looking for Annie Lennox;
what I find is Little Orphan Annie, retired.

In My Daughter's House

"Good air in this house," somebody
says at Salon, not talking
about the cigarette smoke, stopping
a moment between kitchen
and dining room to survey the regular
Friday night hum of hard rock or ballad—
what the dancers will—the earnest
scholarly contemplations—Hegel and Hildegard
of Bingen bumping against job prospects
now that spring brings new degrees more
or less employable, wry tales
of airport (in)security drifting away
into politics and war and is there
any more champagne?
Good air here.

In the kitchen my daughter and I
interrogate a handsome visitor,
suitor (so my mother would have said)
to her youngest but too old for that one,
so we play good cop/bad cop unintentionally.
He responds with candor and aplomb
and gets our message. Would-be
lovers gravitate to the living room,
smokers to the front porch
or the trampoline in back, while the children
who used to fall asleep among coats
only a few years back now race
from room to room in games of hide
and seek and tag, and the only guest my age
claims his favorite beer and chair, and we

observe upon things we both once swore
we'd never talk about—the market,
the world going to hell,
the nature and price of the chemistry
that keeps us viewing with alarm.
Good air here.

The cats, declaring their weekly truce,
have settled in the spare room
but the new stray kitten, uncertain
in her tough-teen-girl disguise,
drifts between dance and trampoline,
sneaking a beer outside. We all pretend
not to notice, though many eyes are
glancing discreetly across the night,
many hands ready, always one
who'll catch her if she falls.
Good air.

We turn out the porch light at two a.m.,
evict nonresidents, order pizza.
The kitten finally
is talking on the trampoline
about the father who threw her out,
the crack house that took her in,
something else—something worse—most of us
have no need to know, but she
has a need to tell. Even before pizza,
she'll hit the couch,
curl up with a warm blanket,

sleep through till late morning.
Good air.

This house is old and moody,
but with the right prompts—bright paints,
string lights, a breath of incense
across Indian shawls and votive candles—
it's regained its sense of humor and begun
to show its gentility, wisdom of years.
Good air tonight in this house.

Scar

I'm thinking of getting a tattoo.
The nearly half-yard sine wave
across my waistline fairly cries out
for adornment.

The family wag suggests a row
of Sherlock-Holmesian dancing men
conga-ing the length, a few falling off
into my navel with a diminishing
Aaieeeeeeeeeee! Someday
I'll take the mark with such grace,

but not yet. I thought of flames—
still one hot mama!—but didn't want
to tempt the gods. Serpent for immortality?
Regretting Eden, I'm afraid of snakes.

I've settled on leaves—blue, I think—
and a nice vine: renewal, but with
a difference, like rue. This scar,
after all, marks an invasion—
complicated: the attack from within,
grave; from without, restoration.

Let these sharp lines sign a return
to innocence, fruit of a new earth, color
of sky, the undreamed place we come
when we have fronted the beast in the field,
surviving.

For Bob on Our 44th Anniversary:
An Appreciation of Time

So here we are again, driving
to a race, trying the roads,
the clocks, the finish lines, as
to a restaurant on Sunday morning
to taste the peace of our time
together; to the big river or beyond
to the ocean to hear tides pulsing
planetary time; to hospitals
and doctors and clinics trusting
in the magic that creates time
as we do ourselves with sheer
determination and a love we never
dreamed the night we shyly
shook hands saying "Howdyedo"
back in a minor election year
before we learned how
on each other's pulse to tell time.

Caribou

None too different from reindeer, I hear,
but do the cows wear antlers?
(The internet story about Santa's team,
it seems, is true.) We're too far south, strange

as that sounds to your average Minnesotan,
to find caribou in the wild,
but there's a coffee shop that claims them
just down the tunnels from the clinic where

every day I slip into the photon beam.
(Also strange and eerie—four long
mosquito whines, hum of fine mechanisms,
and electrons in my chest do silent

jetés, and DNA—mainly the bad, I have
to hope—twists or untwists like a spiral
staircase collapsing, bringing down
the squatter's house. I have to hope.)

After, I find my way through busy halls
to chessboard-painted tables bearing
legends reminding me of flower children—

> *out of the air around us whispers*
> *aroma to our tongues   clouds*
> *of discovery   another may introduce*
> *bright motion*

I understand that no better now than in 1968.

Warming to mocha and a cranberry scone
I pretend I'm still living in the world.

The Music of Christmas

On December 23rd the irradiators
arrive at six a.m. — so many,
the hopeful, the faithful, waiting
for holiday release — and start the ritual,
placing arms, turning hips
a bare millimeter or so, measuring,
setting lasers to sweep
over coordinate tattoos.

The machine stands foursquare behind,
pins the earth, unnoticing, unnoticed
except for its shining appendages,
steely, baffled faces set
to peer as deep almost as the soul,
to send packets of hard x-ray, invisible,
unfelt, hurtling into corporal space.

Somewhere near the far wall, music —

> *Silent night, holy night,*
> *All is calm, all is bright,*

though the closed eye sees nothing;
only the ear hears
a long mosquito whine, the first bolt.

> *'Round yon virgin mother and child,*
> *Holy infant so tender and mild . . .*

An attendant slides new plates
into the glinting face. Its unblinking eye

still peers unmoved, then shifts —

Sleep in heavenly peace,

to a new angle. Again the whine,
longer this time, halfway through.

Sleep in heavenly peace.

A new track, another perspective —

Angels we have heard on high,
Sweetly singing o'er the plains . . .

the third whine sings over
mountains' replies, almost obscures

. . . their joyous strains.
Gloria in excelsis Deo.

After the fourth passover, the machine
discreetly withdraws.

Gloria in excelsis Deo.

Epiphany

My daughter took down her Christmas tree today,
feeling, she said, somehow she'd failed,
had overreacted, expected too much
of this season she has always touched with magic.

What can a mother offer but time?

When her children were young, they flung
themselves into her joy, gasped with delight
at the Advent calendar and the crèche she made,
its lambs and donkey, its shepherd
with his paperclip crook, their own
crafted gauds and baubles.
At story time she read wonders,
and their eyes glowed.

Today, grown but not-grown, they concentrate
on their own stories—this girl, that boy,
a job nagging, a party beckoning. She is still
and is not the center of their whirl,
and they will wander from her
into the labyrinth of their own becoming,
but she will remain the clew.

In time they'll find their way back,
more settled, more experienced,
bringing their own loves to the hearth.
They'll pick up the magic where they dropped it,
for she has been a wise mother,
but for today this dismantling of myth and history
is stuff for tears.

Eye of the Beholder

Mayo Clinic, January 2005

in the hall running
between linear accelerator
and coffee shop
past piano and waterfall
just short of the internet

Miro x 2 both hasty
strokes of black
primary splotches
one something to do with an arrow
the other lines and circles
untitled
but by the 47th pass
I understand parent
and child the small one
wearing an aviator helmet
earflaps hanging

that one leans
pushes nudges burrows
forehead into the tall one's belly
and so they stand an instant
caught for generations the picture
motherfather/sondaughter
content
making me smile

The Chemistry of Sapphire

for Bob on our 45th anniversary

Transparent aluminum oxide, says our book,
anisotropic monoaxial crystal — precise, surely,
yet not so evocative as *celestial jewel,*
royal gem, old guardian
against poisons, demons, and all
the harms that beset kings.
Hard, nearly, as diamond, though rarer.
Truest of blues, but found
in all the sky's colors. Carve
in sapphire the story of faithful
lovers, loyal friends, those who stand
steady against the days. *Grown*
by a heat, our book tells us, the Virgin's
birthstone that marks this anniversary,
that honors our own constant heat,
our fidelity, this fine conservation of years.

Niiji Means Friend

Today we drove up beyond Spooner
to see a man about stars.
While my husband bought a telescope
a dog named in the Ojibwe gave me welcome,
untroubled by the scent of cat.
Transactions made, we drove home
through a perfect September
sky bright as a robin's egg, sun
warm on our faces, telling each other
the sumac had turned early this year.
We laughed at the jokes of years;
I drifted to sleep part-way home
and woke to wild asters at the roadside.
It had been a long time since
we had traveled such a highway
with no one to let blood at the end.

Reading for Hope

for the residents of Hope Lodge, Rochester, Minnesota

They're remarkably attentive, forty
or so people middling young to genuinely
elders with so much else on their minds.
Tuesdays are potluck nights,
and we've eaten well, accent on meats
and potatoes, sauces, good breads—
doubtless their doctors have been urging
"Eat. You're losing too much weight"—
words most never thought to hear.

Some wear the telltale scarf or turban,
one a splendid little hat that makes her
look like a Parisienne *gamine*.
Others show the discreet black dot
tattoo that tells the radiation techs
where to center their beams.
Some show no outward emblem,
only a look—concentration? distraction?
a certain deep seriousness.

When I sat down at the table with my plate
their first question was "What kind
do you have?" It's the bond
we all understand. I've come
as a kind of show-and-tell, recalling
one year past, how I sat with others

just like them and waited
for the entertainment, the half-
hour or so of diversion from the thoughts
that never really leave our minds.

Poetry or comedy or gospel singing—it's all one,
a brief remembrance of the mundane world,
happy forgetting.

Lunches at the Siam Terrace
and Crane Alley

Day One: Zoë

Scarcely able to sit still, so much energy.
We order egg rolls, stir-fry—vegan for her;
I'll have the chicken—with rice and tea.
Lacking the art to read the leaves,
I ask the question she's been expecting,
the one I asked her brother last spring,
nothing major, just *What would you like to do
with the rest of your life?*

Right now she says *I'm doing what I want to,
feeding the poor, protesting
so many injustices in the world. No reason
to look for new directions.*

No time to talk about college now, little
to explore music, food, or love before
she hurries off to an appointment.
I stay behind, finish my tea, wonder
about the story in the bottom of the cup.

Day Two: Faith

Dublin and Paris in the past, Vienna
in the offing. In Chicago a grandfather
wrestling at the brink, able—
or not—to hold on till her return,
but today we talk coursework,
learning the language, the wonder
of negotiating a new Old World.
We share burgers and fries (her vegetarian
mother will be horrified), recognizing
all she leaves behind, looking forward
to *Käse, Bier, und Brötchen* in the spring.
We stroll home under a winter sun,
eyes turning to distance, known words
unspoken in our throats.

Day Three: Shannon

Given enough world and time
we can turn this into a tradition.
We talk of rap and poetry (his, mine),
reflect upon our muses, how they come through,
where falter. (Who would have predicted
out of all we'd be the rhymers?)

Over another day's burgers and fries
he says the art of meats should not
end with me. Making his living
in the kitchen now, he asks
if I'll share my recipes with him.
When I get home I'll email him
some standards, compile a "best
of the rest" for his birthday.

On the way out we talk
about his turning twenty-one.
He says before he goes to college
he wants to drive the country.
I agree he should, cross my fingers,
hope for smooth roads, good tires,
worry a little, knowing the world
not always kind to poets.

Last Night in the 405

The house echoes—with emptiness, of course,
the scattering, possibility. They've been sorting
and packing for four weeks now.
My daughter says she tried thinning
twenty-five years of toys and treasures
but in the end the stories got in the way.

> *Flash back to her at seventeen, stepping*
> *onto a bus for Boulder, earnest*
> *hippie in a long paisley skirt, back-*
> *pack crammed with necessaries,*
> *among them the pink plush bunny.*

Today a neighbor they'd never met
stopped by to say how sorry she was
they were leaving. She'd looked to them,
she said, for pennants and placards and all
the colors of gentle rebellion.

The truck loaded by dinner with everything
except futons—books and bookcases,
plates, glasses, cups, and pans, only
a little furniture—the helpers sat
over pizza and beer remembering
what they loved about this house,
planned visits and emails and Thanks-
givings, clung to the moment, then clung
to one another till the last door closed.

> *When my daughter was fourteen we moved*
> *to a house on the edge of town, our sixth*

home since she'd been born. She objected
to the distance, but liked the pantry
under the stairs, which she declared
a poet's nook. I'm not sure anyone
has ever written a poem there,
but the possibility remains.

At 2:30 the cats got loose—no real crisis
as it turned out, but enough
to start the day—little sleep to follow
until the truck rolled at seven.

The futons went on last. The steel ramp
slid up, doors swung to, surprising quiet.
Cats and computers went by car.

The house is going to two who'll love it.
The road away is amazingly long.

Shadow

Most days you don't notice she's there
even when the sun shines. You put her
out of your mind, but she follows you,
spilling the salt when you scramble eggs,
overfilling the coffeemaker, burning toast.

Sit down with a new book and she reads
over your shoulder, loses your place
when you get up to answer the phone.
Say you're going for a walk, she'll hide
your left shoe. Most of the time

you don't think to blame her, but somehow
you know she's behind you. All you need
is one suspect moment—a new twinge
that repeats itself, a cough that holds on,
ten pounds you didn't really try to lose—

and first, you think you hear her in the hall.
Then you catch glimpses of a wraith
at the edge of vision when you turn your head.
Eventually she camps out at the foot
of your bed watching you chase sleep.

By then even the cat notices.
You begin to consider the odds
you're joining the battle again.

Once More onto the Beaches

Better to have throat
than chest or belly cut

provided it's done right

you'll still breathe and swallow
sweetness in an iron hour

Post-Op

Ten days out and the nerves wake irritable
as any sleeper roused too soon.
What felt like a fine Victorian choker—wide
black velvet, you were thinking, with a simple cameo
or gold filigree—in a breath morphs
to fine barbed wire, and hot.
You're walking in the garden now, relishing
light that promises before long to falter and cool,
reminding yourself to leave that nightshade
that no fence holds back, for anyone else to pull,
never mind its shallow root.
You talk now and then to its cousin tomatoes,
heavy and round and still bright green,
coaxing a *carpe diem* before frost
puts paid to summer's hope.
You measure progress sun to sun, know only
time and tempo, concentrate on slow
breathing and quick senses, eyes open wide
to this transitory cadence of days.

Mall Walking with Valkyries

Trust me, I used to look like that—
long, lean. Dressed all in black too;
sometimes still do. I know as well
how to brave the wind as prowl
this place of commerce.

These days, of course, when I'm alone,
nobody stares at just one more woman
of questionable years looking at sheets
and towels, pricing a garnet pendant
or a leather bag—not much to show
how holy fire still smolders deep down.

But here, the three of us together—
oh, I don't fool myself: heads turn
to watch maid, mother, crone
striding the walkways, navigating crowds,
pausing for mocha at the food court before
moving out on our own mystic business,
but it's those two they see—one
chestnut, the other blonde, subject
to change without notice—bare armed,
broad shouldered, sleek as selkies,
which they both might be, except I know
I bore the one, she the other,
and we claim dry land.

Our allotted hours skim past: we shop,
we buy, we walk, we stop to look.
I lean upon the laughter they bring me.
Touching their fire, I draw strength, my most
treasured commodity to carry home.
Out in the world we understand
Victoria's Secret has nothing on our own.

For Bob on Our 46th Anniversary

Our love is the rush of water
over stone, soothing, gentling,
making the rugged smooth.

Our love is the glow of two
scarlet flowers growing
at the edge of water, brightness,
light even in shadow.

I see you and I catch my breath.

I Discuss Horses with My Oncologist

"Blinkers, not blinders," he says.
"On the draft horses we always
called them blinders," I say,
those bits of bridle that keep their eyes
straight on the business ahead.
"Some horses," he says, "wear only one,
need to see the rail but panic at the sight
of the crowd. Do you know
about the shadow roll," he asks,
"that wide roll of lamb's wool
across the nose?" "Not just decoration?"
"Not at all. Some horses shy on the run
at the shadow of their own front foot.
Brain the size of a walnut." Son
of a man who'd bet the farm,
he shakes his head. I tell him
about Old Queen, smile picturing
feet the size of dinner plates,
back broad and flat as a playing field,
gait like a backyard hammock.
Only thing that ever troubled her
was horseflies. Maybe the difference lies
all in how they—and we—think of time.

Zebra

i.

Old med school rule:
when you hear hoofbeats
think horses, not zebras.

Necessary corollary: Someday
there will come a zebra.

ii.

Most unusual says the wise
woman in the white coat. *Highly
unlikely* another concurs.
My God! thus the gentleman
from another venue, *nobody
gets that!*

Zebra rising.

iii.

Life is not all
(you know this)
black and white,
but zebras are.

Do these two facts
color the way
they see the world?

iv.

Poke flank, prod chest,
look closely at the teeth.

Diagnosis
or zebra trading?

v.

In the comics a crocodile
with extraordinary accent

harangues his zebra neighbor
to come and be eaten.

Zebra demurs. Funny zebra.

vi.

*These chemicals will do
the trick—almost always
work—see here in this book.*

Almost always. . . . Oh.

vii.

In danger
does Zebra take on
the spirit of Lion
pursuing?

viii.

Consulting dictionary
of terms known only
to the initiated:

Z (Ger. *Zucking*) contraction

Zeatin toxin that can be
    made from sweet corn

Zelotypia excessive zeal
    or jealousy

Zieve's syndrome the ultimate
    among hangovers

No *zebra*.

ix.

Strange, beautiful,

in some locations
threatened with extinction,

asking only forage
and freedom—
essence of zebra.

x.

Teflon and steel—
exotic trees—how many
make a forest?

Beyond the glass grass
murmurs under light
rain.

xi.

Cats in the dark
all, they say, are gray.

Do zebras running
strobe in moonlight?

xii.

Scalpels:
Little's and general
and Mayo operating,
Liston and Bistoury,
even ultrasonic.

Zebras among knives.

xiii.

Online fine example
of the photographer's art:
Lion attacks, Zebra
escapes on motorcycle.

Go, Zebra!

Nadine S. St. Louis was born and raised outside Silverton, Oregon, in the Cascade foothills, and has lived in Minneapolis, Baltimore, and Los Angeles, but for more than half her life she has called Eau Claire, Wisconsin, home. She has worked as a legal secretary and circuit court clerk in Eugene, Oregon; taught English as a Second Language for a short time at the University of Minnesota; and for a much longer time taught English literature and composition at the University of Wisconsin-Eau Claire, specializing in the 17th and 27th centuries—Shakespeare, John Donne, and science fiction—but she came late to the writing of poetry. A year-long faculty exchange in Bielefeld, Germany, gave her both the time and inspiration. Since then, her poetry and reviews have appeared in numerous publications including *ByLine, Free Verse, Kalliope, Kaleidoscope,* and the *Literary Magazine Review,* as well as multimedia shows in *The Vision and the Word* series and the *Epidemic Peace Project.* Her chapbook *Weird Sisters* appeared in 2000. She is one of the founders of the Chippewa Valley Book Festival.